Watering

Dead

Flowers

Deunvion Smith

now i get it.

nothing is ever going to change until i make change happen.

i've been watering dead flowers in friendships, within myself, and in relationships for a while now…

but i’m done. i’m done putting time and energy into expired things.

i’m ready to let go and heal.

contents

trigger warning

talk of:

negative thoughts and depression

harassment

emotional abuse

body image and appearance

manipulation

you before me

i don’t know myself without you.

my whole world revolved around you so now that you're gone,

i am completely lost.

when i had to choose between myself and you,

i gladly chose you every time.

i was deprived of so much while we were together.

i forgot how to build relationships with other people
and

i forgot how to build a relationship with myself.

the way you made me feel reminded me that i was alive

but tore me down at the same time.

it felt good feeling the pain of losing you because it made me realize

i was capable of feeling.

i still remember the pain of going through those sleepless nights but to me,

it was worth it.

loving you is like throwing seeds on dry dirt and

waiting for flowers to grow with no water.

lookalike

i look for you in other people.

i look for your smile and your sweet words.

i look for the way you walk, the way you dress, and the way you do your hair.

no matter how much i try to replace you, i can't.

they're just not *you.*

you asked for all of me, and i gave that to you... with just some left for me.

the some i could hold onto in case you decided to leave with the rest.

the some that would pull me up and, on my feet again if anything went wrong.

if this is what love feels like, i don't want it.

the overthinking, the chest pains,

the insomnia, the days without eating

and the discomfort, then i don't want it.

i find beauty in being comfortably naked around
someone.

not naked unclothed, naked in the sense of revealing
myself

and being able to be vulnerable with someone.

having them feel the warmth of my words and
finding comfort in my presence.

fully clothed but naked.

me, the garden

you had a garden full of flowers that you didn't know how to take care of.

yes, you gave me sunlight but what about water?

you didn't take care of me when you had the chance.

now the next person has to water me, in hopes that i'll grow again.

it took me a while to realize that

what i thought was love

was just an attachment.

i can't take it anymore.

all the back and forth.

one minute your foot is in the door, begging for another chance,

then you're slamming the door in my face as you walk out.

chasing unrequited love

i’m tired.

my feet hurt, my legs burn, and i’m so tired.

i’m done chasing after you.

my feelings are not a game.

every time i’m ready to give up, you stop and give me hope that we can someday be together, only to pick up speed again and leave.

i love you less and less when you do that.

why our relationship didn’t work out

is the first and last thing on my mind everyday.

we were so close yet so far away from each other.

sometimes i feel like we could hear each other screaming to

get out of the relationship but we just ignored each other.

are we fixing this friendship because this is what we both want?

or are we fixing this just because of all the years we put into it?

i hope when we see each other again,

we'll still love each other the same.

he always sees the good in people,

even if they truly are bad people.

i admire him.

he is who i want to grow into.

my overthinking killed our story.

it told me that you didn’t like me for me

and that you deserved better.

home

i set fire to the place i went to for comfort and stability.

to the place where peace and love stayed.

i set fire to the place that loved me unconditionally

and that gave me shelter whenever i needed it.

i knew from the beginning how our story would end.

it wasn't built on a good foundation.

our story wasn't set up for a happy ending.

you will always be here as my first love but when i look around, you're not the first person i see before everyone else.

i don't look for you and compare what you can do to others.

you were once my moon, now you're just a star.

i could fill up this whole book talking about him.

i would talk about how pretty and loved he made me feel

and how sweet and caring he is.

i could go on for days about how his voice and laughter kept me sane,

and how his existence kept me alive.

she started to drift away.

i could tell it was coming to an end, but i didn't want to lose her so,

i kept pulling and pulling.

i didn't know that would push her further away.

- *his pov*

at 2am when your mind can't stop racing,

and counting sheep doesn't work,

can you think of us to get you to sleep?

it's hard loving you and myself at the same time.

i stayed.

i stayed until i had nothing left to give you.

until i, myself, was gone.

you give me everything i need just by existing and loving me wholeheartedly.

i feel guilty for putting my needs first and ending the relationship.

i feel like i should've stayed and just stuck it out.

i feel like with time, it would've gotten better.

while i was starting to feel good,

you felt bad and that's becoming hard to live with everyday.

you were sweet to me.

you treated me like i was delicate, and i found the one i fell in love with inside of you.

i found happiness and fulfillment.

i was happy to wake up with the sun.

i'd do anything to go back to december.

you were kind to me and i'm forever grateful for you.

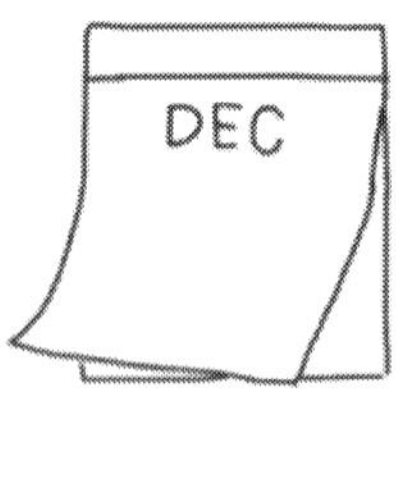

my insecurities were your desires and to this day, i still don't understand why.

how could you look at someone like me and love me without a second thought?

how could you not be embarrassed by me?

and of course, when his pretty face told me those pretty words, i believed him.

love

/ləv/

noun

1. a word i throw around often without really understanding the meaning or feeling of.

my first ~~love~~ fixation

writing takes the form of whatever new is in my life at the time and

this time, right now, it's you. all my diary pages are filled with you.

i would like to believe that i have more to write about and maybe

i do but right now, it's just you.

it's sad how much power you have over my mind,

but i know that once you're gone,

my writing will take the form of someone or something else and

i'll forget all about you.

allowing myself to be fully vulnerable with you is
something i can't do yet.

the thought of you turning my vulnerability against
me is my biggest fear.

i love you but you make me feel bad.

you keep me up at night with tears in my eyes and

negative thoughts in my head.

communication

something that wasn't part of the relationship.

something that was non-existent.

something that ended us.

i would say that i hope to see you again later in life,

but i don’t think that’s true.

i think i never want to see you again.

i think we all deserve someone who makes us want to live our days to the fullest and

not want to give up.

someone who brings out the best in us and

helps us fix the not so pretty parts.

the way you love is suffocating.

i'm not able to love you the way you want me to and

i'm sorry.

to die loving you would make death

seem not so scary.

and that's the problem.

i should be afraid of death, who isn't?

i should die having experienced all that life has to offer, not just experiencing you.

we needed each other to be more.

we needed each other to feel more.

i think we just needed more than each other at the time.

i wanted to be in love.

i wanted to feel loved.

because of this, i ignored all the signs of you holding me back.

for so long i tried to mold you into the person i wanted you to be. i tried to change you to fit my story and you did the same to me but that's not how love works. this chapter of the book, our chapter, is over. it's time for me to say goodbye now. i'm putting down my pen. there's nothing else to write or say, our time has come to an end.

feelings

i don’t know how i feel.

it's like i feel it all, but i feel nothing at all.

i feel the hurt in my heart that my mind tells me not to feel.

my mind tells me to act out while my heart tells me to stay calm.

i’m at war with myself.

you make me feel horrible for reacting to the pain that you cause.

i'm listening to your problems but what about mine?

i'm always there to help you off the side of the cliff

while you leave me there hanging, every time.

i was left there to fall into the depths of my thoughts
once again

with no guidance out.

i guess you could say i'm a collector.

i like collecting books (especially love ones),

pictures of the moon and stars,

memories (sad and happy ones), and love.

i like collecting love from people around me.

being loved is such a nice feeling.

i was in a bad place and felt so alone.

no one noticed.

i know that after i get done crying,

i'll have to go ask for forgiveness for all the hurtful things i said while i was in pain.

i'm not afraid of this dark hole anymore.

i embrace it now.

i'm making friends here.

i failed. i'm a failure.

i haven't reached the level of success that i told myself i should've reached by now.

i'm scared because the window of opportunity i gave myself is closing

and i haven't accomplished anything yet.

i've been working hard with nothing to show for it.

this consumes my thoughts.

how much more are you going to take?

i'm running out and soon i will have nothing left for myself.

days feel like months, and minutes like hours.

my days are blurring and i'm losing track of time.

i space out and come back to myself completely lost and behind.

the showers are getting longer and hotter again and the meals are getting shorter.

i'm losing myself and falling into old habits.

i’ll wake up and go on about my day.

i’ll wave at you, i’ll smile, and i’ll laugh but

i can’t promise you anything after the sun sets.

how sad is dying without ever experiencing happy tears?

experiencing something so joyful and meaningful that

all you can do is cry is something i want to experience.

i want to be so happy that i find myself dancing around in the kitchen at 3am

or so happy that pausing and taking a deep breath won't feel like a chore anymore.

i want the type of happiness that lets me throw my negative perspectives out the window

and just live.

i feel like i'm being held hostage by my own mind and body.

i'm a prisoner of depression. not being able to move or speak until it's ready.

wanting to call out for help but being stopped by the voice in my head telling me no one is coming to save me.

wanting the pain to stop but at the same time needing it to stay because it’s a reminder that i'm not dead yet.

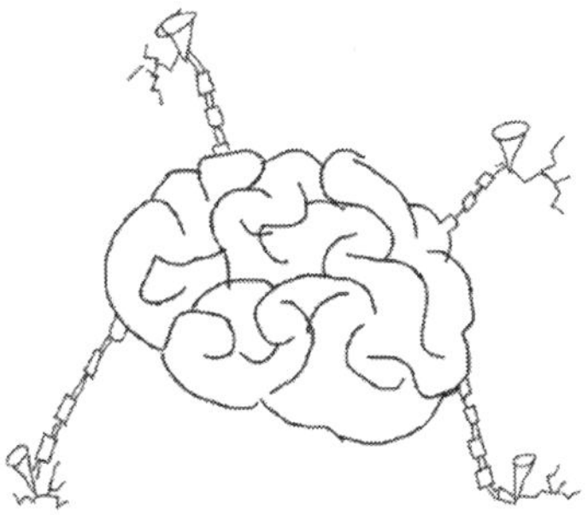

finding peace and comfort in being alone is hard.

i want so badly to find someone from my past to occupy my time with.

i want to get sucked back into their old ways just to not feel alone anymore.

for the first time in a while, it happened.

the feeling was almost unfamiliar.

the walls caved in, and it got dark.

it took me a minute to figure out what was happening but soon, i remembered the feeling all too well.

my confidante and my neighbor but also my worst enemy,

depression.

it was back.

all i see are blank canvases.

others around me see art.

they see the canvas full of color and full of life, but i see nothing.

i just see a blank, white canvas.

i was so nude about my feelings.

i think that's why it hurt so much.

you listened to me cry.

you listened to the pain in my voice as i screamed

and you still walked away.

they have made themselves comfortable.

my mind feeds me negative thoughts all day about my friends, family, and about myself.

i walk around in a bad mood wondering why when i'm the reason why.

i manifest them.

i let them get comfortable.

i let them control my mood and my actions.

i let them control me.

i've never felt farther away from myself

than i do right now.

i'm not at ease

and i don't think my mind will ever let me be.

it will always remember the times i was at my lowest

and no one seemed to notice.

no matter how many apologizes i get or sympathetic looks,

i will never be at ease with the dark times i went through

with no one by my side.

sadness consumes me and feeds me at the same time.

it wraps me up in a blanket and gives me comfort

while tearing me down.

i don’t know what to do on days like these.

days when everything starts off good and then it just isn't.

days when my body shuts down and my brain starts yelling.

days when all i want to do is stay in bed and cry.

days when my mind feeds me negative thoughts so bad,

i feel like laying in that dark hole i call depression and giving up.

what do i do on days like these?

i know life is precious and should be filled with memories and

moments of happiness, but i can't enjoy it because

life keeps getting in the way of me living.

i've been watering dead flowers inside of myself. feeding into the negative thoughts and being comfortable with where me and depression stand but i'm done now. i'm tired of letting depression take over my mind, my body, and my life. i want out of this hole and i'm going to do everything in my power to get out of it. i'm not giving up.

self

i fear people viewing me how i view myself.

them viewing me as weak, as too sensitive, as an easy target

because of my low self-esteem, and viewing me as all around,

too much to handle.

my younger self needs my help but i’m not ready to confront her yet.

i’m not ready to sit down with her and talk about the past.

i’m not ready to heal her because healing her means confronting things i’ve worked hard to hide.

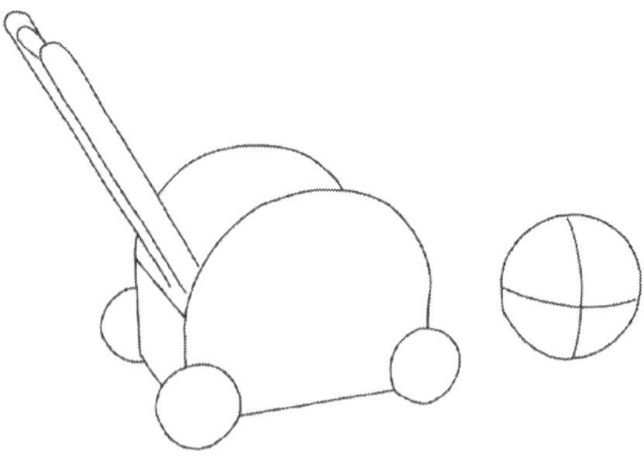

i forgive you for not having my back.

i forgive you for making me look like a fool defending you.

i forgive you for leaving.

i forgive you for hurting my feelings.

i forgive you but i never want to see or talk to you again.

love, your daughter

how can you say you love and care about me then run back to the source of my pain?

how could you still care about someone who hurt me?

this is such a confusing time.

i don't want to be me anymore.

i don't want to do this anymore.

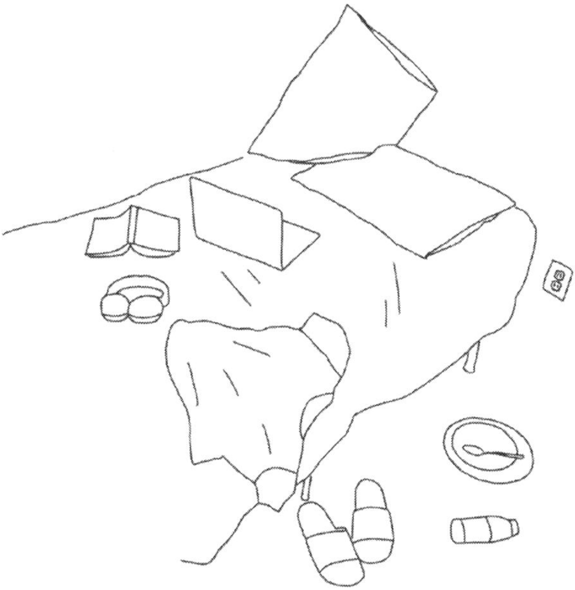

you wanted someone you could control.

someone without a mind of their own.

someone who would rather die than

be without you but that wasn't me.

i had goals that exceeded you and you hated that.

i want to be accepted without comment for change.

i want to be loved, truly loved and appreciated.

i want to be the person they pick out of a room full of people.

i want to be sure about myself and the things i can do.

i want to be understood.

i'm not dramatic.

what you did and said hurt me.

but why? why am i so emotional?

why do i let your words cut me and drain me dry?

maybe if i wasn't so open to making friends that year...

maybe if i wasn't so quick to brush it off as nothing...

maybe if i wasn't so nice to him...

maybe if i wasn't so weak and afraid to speak up for myself...

then maybe, none of it would've happened.

i did it all for love and acceptance but in the end, it still wasn’t enough.

<u>you don't know sorry</u>

i'm tired of accepting apologies from people who are never going to change.

i'm tired of being treated badly then being told to forgive and move on.

why is hurting me so normal to you?

do you keep doing it because you know i'll forgive you in the end?

do i need to change or do you?

avoiding mirrors is something i have become good at.

seeing what people see when they look at me is something that terrifies me.

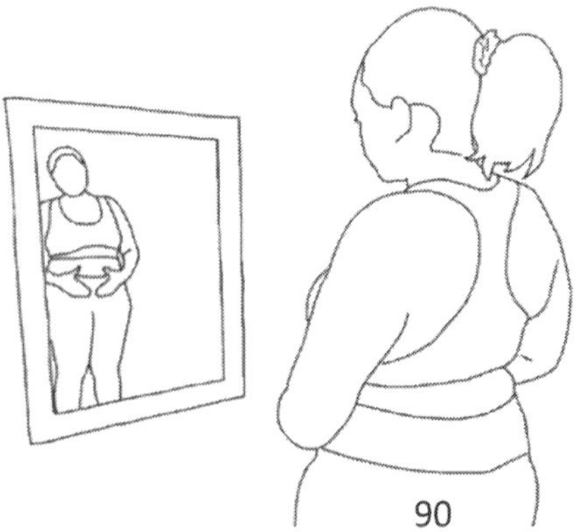

i'll take this anger out on you,

i'll take it out on the walls of my room,

and i'll take it out on myself because,

i would rather hurt myself and the people i love than
tell you that i hate you.

i don’t think i should feel obligated to love you

just because of the place you hold in my life.

you’re a terrible liar.

you would think that after years,

you’d be better at it.

i was so pathetic

waiting around for phone calls after every big life event.

i was so pathetic

throwing all my love at you and you stepping right over it

but me still standing by saying “he’ll come back for it” ... you never did.

i was so pathetic

waiting on those “i'm proud of you” calls.

i was so pathetic

i know you love me but it's not enough.

i need more.

mind

i'll give into your manipulation.

i'll let you put negative thoughts in my head.

i'll let you control me.

feelings

i'll let you control how i feel today.

i'll listen to the words you say and they will determine my mood.

i want to be the type of attractive that you read about in books and see in romance movies.

you know, the type that everyone stops and stares at,

the type that every guy wants but every guy can't have.

i want to be the type that someone would sit and write poetry about.

i want to be the type of attractive that you find attractive.

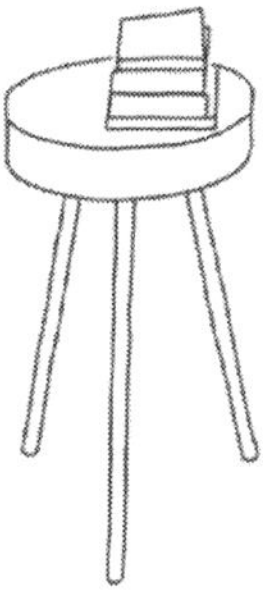

you made me feel like i wasn’t enough.

you made me feel worthless.

you made me, as your child, feel like i was a burden.

don’t give up on me yet.

whatever you want me to be, i can be it.

i'll do any and everything

but love myself for you to accept me.

i want my legs to stop shaking and my heart to stop pounding every time a man walks into the room.

i want to not have thoughts of getting hurt or thinking of ways to safely exit just in case.

i want to not have to look over my shoulder every few seconds.

i want to feel safe.

the first to let me down were my thoughts,

the perception of myself, *myself*.

you make me feel stupid for wanting your love and attention.

you make me feel like i don’t deserve it and it has to be earned.

i thought you changed.

i thought things were going to be different this time.

when you had to choose, you never chose me.

to: life, myself and family

i both love and hate you at the same time.

i let what people say take over my life and have me question everything

while they keep on living.

why do i do that?

he was a way better person in the letters and

in birthday cards than in real life.

i hate this part of getting older.

the part where everything starts to look smaller,

where everything is final, and where the things that once made me smile and laugh, are too childish to do now.

when he ignored how i felt and what i was saying,

i was a kid again, trying to get my parents to
understand me.

i never thought i deserved nice things like having pretty clothes, having my hair done, or even wearing makeup.

i always thought that none of that would matter on an "ugly body".

until i learned that there was no such thing as an "ugly body" just an ugly society

with ugly mindsets and ugly words.

i can't love in this environment.

love is not taught here, love is not shown here, and love does not grow here.

i still feel the same way i felt all those years ago when i called this place a house and not a home.

i think it's time to move on and look for the love i've been craving

somewhere else.

i have to be careful when i have a moment of happiness.

if someone sees, all my cries for help will be turned into lies.

<u>like father</u>

comparing me to him hurts.

do you really see him inside of me?

how could you compare me to someone like that?

while down this road of self-love and discovery,

i've found nothing but more hatred for myself.

for some reason, the thought of loving myself
disgusts me.

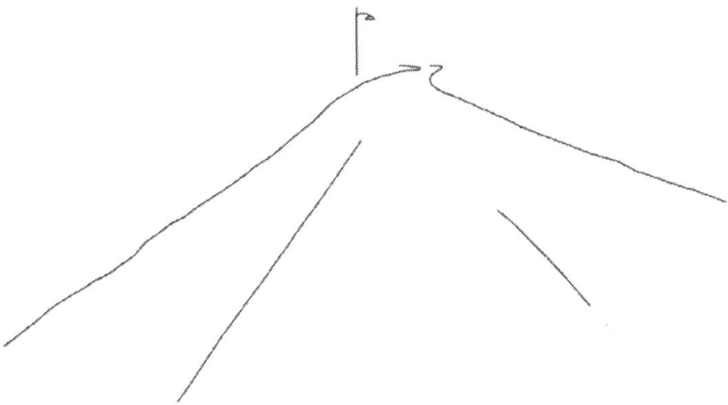

i fear rejection.

i fear it in relationships,

i fear it from my family members,

i fear it from friends,

and i fear it from my parents.

i fear rejection from everyone.

i fear it from society

and i fear it from myself.

i don’t practice self-care.

it’s a luxury i don’t think i deserve.

i'm ready to heal. forgiving is hard but i'm ready to let go and forgive all of those who hurt me. i'm done planting seeds in environments where they cannot grow. i'm ready to let go of the past and grow instead of staying around those who bring nothing but pain into my life.

for you

it's okay to cry.

it's okay to feel.

cry it out and feel what you need to feel in that moment.

just don’t stay there for too long.

stop letting people who know nothing about you affect the way you feel about yourself.

don’t go looking for love in places where love
cannot and will not grow.

you have to water yourself.

don't wither up and die, waiting for someone to come along and do it for you.

get out of your head.

your negative thoughts are holding you back.

sometimes taking a break and distancing yourself can be a good thing.

we get so invested in others and their happiness

that we forget to invest and do things to make us happy.

you deserve all the time and energy that you give to others.

stop hurting yourself for love.

love shouldn’t hurt and love shouldn’t be forced.

don’t feel obligated to stay because of how many months or years you’ve been with your person.

if you are unhappy, leave.

choose yourself.

allow yourself to grow with the comfort of yourself.

find someone who will call you beautiful twenty times a day

and reassure you whenever you're feeling insecure.

don't let your past and things that hurt you

define who you are.

you need to surround yourself with people who are going to help you grow

and who are willing to grow with you.

who are going to water you daily and who won't give up on you.

set yourself as a beauty standard and learn to love yourself above all.

we get older and our bodies change, learn to love the you that you are now

and the you that you might become later in life.

start learning how to heal without an apology.

that person may never apologize, and you don't want to be stuck waiting for them to come around and give you one.

you should never feel guilty for letting go of a friendship or relationship

that does not serve you purpose anymore.

how to stop watering dead flowers

1. learn to notice when the flowers are dying. realize that the relationship is coming to an end with that person.
2. stop going back to check. i know it took a while to grow the flower but when you're done, be done.
3. stop wasting time and energy on the dead ones and go plant new ones. in the process, start watering yourself.

you deserve someone who will show you off in a gallery full of people instead of keeping you hidden away in a dark room.

find yourself before looking for your moon.

find out what you like and what you don't like.

find yourself before looking for a partner so when the time comes, setting boundaries will be easy for you to do.

take all the time you need.

when you come back to yourself, we'll all be here waiting for you.

don't forget that when the lights went out, and you ran to them for comfort,

you found them standing there with the broken light beside them.

remember that before you think about going back to them.

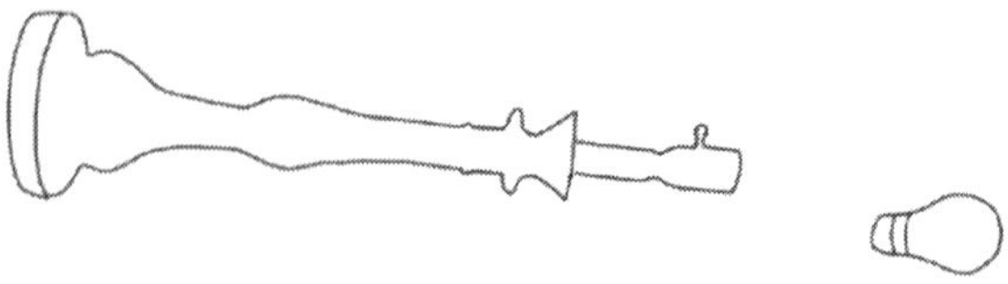

create your own story with you as the main character.

be your own love interest.

stop watering dead flowers in friendships and relationships.

if you are always the one reaching out and always the one trying to fix situations on their behalf, it might be time to start doing some thinking.

on days you don’t feel like getting up for the day,
don’t force yourself to.

take all the time you need to rest and recharge.

take these words of advice and use them in your life.
use them to reassure yourself when no one else will
and use them to reassure others.

don’t let your life revolve around them. there are
many other flowers out there. stop watering those
who are already dead and who aren’t willing to grow
again. i know it’s hard. letting go of someone that
you want to fix and want to help change can be hard.
i know you want to keep believing that they really
are going to change but when is enough, enough?

cover art and illustrations by:

Deunvion Smith

other books by Deunvion Smith:

because you exist, i write

Printed in Great Britain
by Amazon

30638140R00083